INFORMATION EXPLORER

SUPER SMART INFORMATION STRATEGIES

USING DIGITAL IMAGES

by Suzy Rabbat

CHERRY LAKE PUBLISHING • ANN ARBOR, MICHIGAN

CHERRY LAKE Publishing

Published in the United States of America
by Cherry Lake Publishing
Ann Arbor, Michigan
www.cherrylakepublishing.com

Content Adviser: Gail Dickinson, PhD,
Associate Professor, Old Dominion University,
Norfolk, Virginia

Book design and illustration: The Design Lab

Photo credits: Cover, ©iStockphoto.com/STAMIK; pages 3 and 21, ©iStockphoto.com/Imo; page 4, ©iStockphoto.com/kaisersosa67; page 5, ©iStockphoto.com/ricardoreitmeyer; page 9, ©iStockphoto.com/DanBrandenburg; page 10, ©iStockphoto.com/ShaneKato; page 11, ©iStockphoto.com/tzooka; pages 15 and 22, Photo courtesy of NASA; page 17, ©iStockphoto.com/ugurhan; pages 18 and 19, ©iStockphoto.com/filo; page 20, ©iStockphoto.com/DaddyBit; page 23 left, ©iStockphoto.com/inhauscreative; page 23 right, ©iStockphoto.com/Jbryson; page 24, ©Shmel/Shutterstock, Inc.; page 26, ©Olga Lyubkina/Shutterstock, Inc.; page 29, ©iStockphoto.com/ansaj

Library of Congress Cataloging-in-Publication Data
Rabbat, Suzy.
   Super smart information strategies. Using digital images/by Suzy Rabbat.
       p. cm.—(Information explorer)
   Includes bibliographical references and index.
   ISBN-13: 978-1-60279-954-7 (lib.bdg.)
   ISBN-13: 978-1-61080-265-9 (pbk.)
   1. Photography—Digital techniques—Juvenile literature. 2. Digital images—Juvenile literature. I. Title. II. Series.
   TR267.R33 2010   2010018941
   775—dc22

Cherry Lake Publishing would like to acknowledge the work of The Partnership for 21st Century Skills. Please visit *www.21stcenturyskills.org* for more information.

Printed in the United States of America
Corporate Graphics Inc.
July 2011
CLFA09

A NOTE TO PARENTS AND TEACHERS: Please remind your children how to stay safe online before they do the activities in this book.

A NOTE TO KIDS: Always remember your safety comes first!

Table of Contents

CHAPTER ONE
The Basics

⌐ Digital photos can liven up your projects.

Picture this! You are charting the results of your science experiment. You must show the effects of acid rain on the growth of plants. Sure, you could graph your results. But why not bring your findings to life? Track your results with digital photos!

Digital images are images that have been converted into a computer-friendly format. They are saved as image files. Working with digital images is easy once you understand the basics. Let's get started!

A mosaic is a picture that is made up of many colored tiles. The tiles are placed in a pattern to create the image. When you admire a mosaic from a distance, you can easily recognize the design or image. If you take a closer look, you see rows of colored tiles sitting side by side. The placement of the colored tiles is what defines the image. Digital images are like mosaics. Instead of tiles, they're made of small dots or squares. These dots or squares are called pixels.

The size of a digital image is measured in pixels. An image that is 1800 x 1200 means it is 1800 pixels wide by 1200 pixels high. That's equal to approximately 6 inches (15.2 centimeters) wide by 4 inches (10.2 cm) high when printed.

Can you see the pixels when the digital image is enlarged?

TRY THIS!

Let's take a look at pixels. Open a digital image on a computer. Look for the zoom button in the toolbar near the image. This button is often represented by a plus (+) sign. Select the zoom button and enlarge the image. Enlarge it several times. Do you see square-shaped pixels? Can you see how all of the squares come together to create an image?

Larger image files have more pixels. They also have a higher resolution. The resolution is the number of pixels that make up the picture.

High-resolution pictures are sharper than low-resolution pictures. But there are advantages and disadvantages to using both types. See the chart below for more information. It will help you decide which resolution is best for your project.

HIGH RESOLUTION	LOW RESOLUTION
The file is large. The image will be sharp, especially if you want to make a large print.	The file is small. If you try to make a large print, it will look fuzzy or pixelated.
Because the file is big, it takes up a lot of space when stored in your camera or computer.	Low-resolution files won't take up much space in a camera or computer hard drive. You can store more files in less space.
High-resolution images may take a long time to download and view on a Web site.	Low-resolution images are easier to share with others on the Web or in an email.

All digital pictures are made of pixels. They come in different packages or formats. The format tells the computer how to read or open the file. Here are some common formats for digital images:

- The JPEG format is very popular for photos. Because JPEG files can show millions of colors, they make digital photos look real. JPEGs can also be reduced to make the file smaller without losing the quality of the picture.
- Two other common formats are PNG and GIF files. These files are usually small in size. They are commonly used for images that are drawn, such as clip art.

TRY THIS!

Open an Internet browser. Do an image search for pictures of dogs. You should find photos and clip art images. With an adult's permission, save some images to the desktop. Look closely at the end of each file name. The letters that come after the dot (.) identify the type of file. Can you tell which images are JPEGs, GIFs, or PNGs?

CHAPTER TWO
Capturing Images

We've learned that digital images come in different sizes and file formats. Now let's discover how to capture the perfect image for your project.

Digital cameras are great tools for documenting projects that develop over time, such as science experiments. Digital cameras also help record special events, such as class field trips. Taking good digital photos is easy if you keep these points in mind:

1. **Rule of Thirds:** The subject of your photo is what you want people to pay attention to. It may be a person, animal, building, or whatever you like. Think before you click. Where will the subject appear in your photo? You may want to place the subject in the center. There are other options, especially if the background helps tell the photo's story.

Using the Rule of Thirds will help you take more professional-looking photos.

One guide to help you frame shots is called the Rule of Thirds. Picture a grid of nine boxes arranged in three rows and three columns. Imagine that grid over the image you see in the camera's viewfinder. Put your subject anywhere the imaginary lines intersect. Consider what will appear in the background. Is it something that adds interest to your picture? If so, be sure to include it. The idea behind the Rule of Thirds is to place the subject along the outer third of the image. Is the background cluttered? If so, your audience may have a hard time determining what's important to look at. Test different setups before shooting.

2. **Lighting:** The sun or natural light is often best for shooting photos. Where you shoot in relation to the sun's position is important. Imagine shooting an image of a friend when the sun is directly behind you. Your subject may squint. You may find that the best setup is to have the sun to the side of your subject.

3. **Point of View:** Be creative with your shots. Try shooting from different angles. Capture your subject from above and below. Zoom in or zoom out. If you're shooting photos of a small child, try getting down to her eye level. Capture the world from her point of view.

Taking a photo into the sun makes the subject a silhouette.

Keep it steady! If you want sharp, clear photos, it's important to hold the camera still. Even a small movement when you click the shutter button can result in a blurry picture. And remember: Don't block the lens with your fingers when you shoot!

TRY THIS! ↷

Digital photography gives you the freedom to shoot many photos. You can keep the ones you like and simply delete the ones you don't. The best way to polish your skills is to practice. Take lots of photos. Explore all the possibilities of framing your pictures. Need a subject? One option is a pet. If you don't have one, ask if you can shoot images of a friend's or family member's pet.

As you shoot, be sure to
1. take shots from many different angles;
2. zoom in and out to different degrees;
3. make use of the Rule of Thirds for at least some of the images.

Did you come up with some amazing shots?

Suppose you are doing a report on the Pyramids of Giza. You probably can't take your own digital photos of the pyramids. Luckily, you can probably find some online.

Google™

pyramids

SEARCH

TRY THIS!

Practice finding digital images online. Use a search engine such as Google SafeSearch for Kids (www.safesearchkids.com). Enter the Keywords or phrase in the search field for the image you need. You could enter pyramids as an example. Click on one of the links in your search results. Look for pictures that match your search. Save or drag the images to your desktop.

continued ⟶

Pyramid Images

continued →

When you've found several images, create a folder on your desktop. Give it a clear title. "Pyramid Images" is one example. You may want to create more folders within that general folder, depending on how many images you find. For example, you could create two folders within the "Pyramid Images" folder. You could save one as "Outside Shots" and the other as "Inside Shots." Taking the time to organize your images as you collect them is important. You'll be glad you did when the time comes to decide how to use them in your project!

Remember to be a responsible user of information. All images have a source. A source is the creator or owner of the image. Always cite the source of your images. Include this information in your citation:

- Name of the photographer (if available)
- Title or description of the image
- The word *image* in parentheses
- Title of the Web page
- Web address or URL
- Date you downloaded the image file

YOUR CITATION SHOULD LOOK LIKE THIS:

photographer   image description

Bean, Alan. "Conrad unfurls flag" (image). Available from: NASA GRIN: Great Images in NASA <grin.hq.nasa.gov/ ABSTRACTS/GPN-2000-001104.html> (accessed 30 Apr 2010).

date

title of Web site and URL

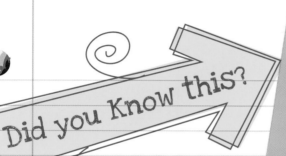
Did you know this?

There are millions of images on the Internet. Many images are protected by copyright. They should not be used without permission. The copyright protection means an image is the intellectual property of the person who created it. Do you want to include online images in your school project? Here are some guidelines to follow:

Government organizations such as NASA often have copyright-free photos on their Web sites. .

1. Search for images on sites labeled copyright free or royalty free.
2. If the site is not copyright free, use no more than five images from one artist or photographer. Use no more than 10% or 15 images, whichever is less, from a collection.

3. You can also contact whoever owns the rights to the photo and ask for permission to use it. Look for an email address on the site. Send a message explaining how and why you would like to use the image.

Sheetfed scanners
are useful for
scanning documents.

A scanner is a tool for creating digital images. A document scanner is one type of scanner. It scans or "reads" the words and images on a document. Scanning a document is like taking a picture of it. The scanner is connected to your computer and creates a digital file as it reads the document. The file can be saved to your computer. Two common types of scanners are sheetfed scanners and flatbed scanners.

Sheetfed scanners are used to scan single documents. This type of scanner is useful for turning documents such as special certificates into digital images.

Flatbed scanners can be used to scan documents and much more. To use a flatbed scanner, lift the cover. Place a document facedown on the glass plate and close the cover. The scanner uses light reflected through the glass to read the text and images. A flatbed scanner can also be used to scan items that are not single sheets of paper. You can digitize things such as the program

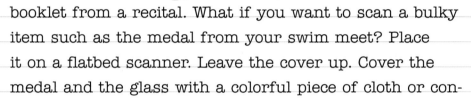

Flatbed scanners can scan almost anything.

booklet from a recital. What if you want to scan a bulky item such as the medal from your swim meet? Place it on a flatbed scanner. Leave the cover up. Cover the medal and the glass with a colorful piece of cloth or construction paper. This will provide a background for your digital image while keeping the scanner light contained.

Scanners can also be used to make digital images of old photographs. These images can then be used in a family tree or digital scrapbook. You can even scan your own original artwork. Then you could use the digital images to make cards or calendars as special gifts.

17

CHAPTER THREE
Photo Editing

Digital pictures can be changed or modified to fit your needs. Most word processing applications have built-in tools for editing images. Let's look at some ways to edit your digital images.

Maybe you want to draw attention to something important in a photo. Perhaps you want to remove part of the image. Cropping an image lets you do just that! When you crop a photo, you trim the edges. The cropping tool allows you to select the portion of the image you want to keep. Everything outside the selected area will be removed.

Photo editing software lets you crop a photo with one click.

The Rotate tool is also helpful. It allows you to turn an image. Suppose you have a photo of your friend standing under a tree. But when you insert the photo in a document, it is sideways. It looks as though the tree and your friend are lying on the ground. You can use the Rotate commands to correct the image.

If your image is sideways, you will need to rotate the image 90 degrees.

You can transform your digital photos into works of art using photo editing software. These computer programs make it possible to go beyond the basic editing of cropping and rotating. With most photo editing programs you can create one image with several layers.

Ever wonder what you would look like on the cover of your favorite magazine? Photo editing software can help you find out!

THIS YEAR'S WINNER

$4.75

FAVORITE HIGH SCHOOL TEAMS

SPORTS

Imagine you've written a report about giraffes. With photo editing software, you could visually show their amazing height. First, you would find a photo of a giraffe online. Then, you could ask someone to take a photo of you standing against a solid-colored background. Using photo editing tools, you could remove the background from your photo. Think about how tall you are and how tall the average giraffe is. Where would your head be in relation to the giraffe? With this in mind, you could then layer your image over the giraffe image. Place yourself on the ground standing next to the giraffe. Then you could insert this image in your report. Do you see how digital images can be used to spice up projects? Let's learn about more fun ways to use digital images.

CHAPTER FOUR

Let the Fun Begin!

There are many ways to use digital images in school and personal projects. The creative possibilities are endless!

Keep two things in mind when working with documents and images: text wrap and image size. Text wrapping is a feature in most word processing programs. It allows words to wrap around an image. After you insert an image into a word processing program, look for the text wrap settings. You may be able to choose from several wrap styles. Without formatting the text wrap, your image may end up in a spot where you don't want it. It may even appear in the middle of a word.

Notice how the text on this page wraps around the flower.

TRY THIS!

Give the text wrap tool a try. Open a blank word processing document. Type several sentences. Next, insert an image. With the image selected, look for the image formatting tools. Apply the text wrap format to your image. This should allow you to move the image anywhere on the page.

You may also need to resize the image to make it fit better on the page. To do this, select the image. Drag one of the corners toward the center of the image. Do you see how text wrapping and image resizing can give your document a more polished look?

In 1969, Neil Armstrong became the first man to walk on the moon. While taking the first steps, he said, "That's one small step for a man, one giant leap for mankind." This made people very proud. The moon landing was a great success. Many people still remember Armstrong's famous words today.

Armstrong's trip to the moon is known as the *Apollo 11* mission. There were also two other astronauts on the mission. Their names are Buzz Aldrin and Michael Collins. Aldrin was the second man to walk on the moon. He was in the landing ship with Armstrong. Michael Collins stayed in a ship that orbited the moon. His job was to help Armstrong and Aldrin go back to Earth when the mission was over.

Text wrap makes your documents look neat and organized.

Be sure to resize your image from the corners. This keeps the height and width in proportion. If you don't, your image may become distorted.

Need some ideas for projects that involve using digital images and word processing software? Here are a few:

Greeting Cards: Experiment with digital images and the WordArt tool in Microsoft Word. Create special thank-you notes or party invitations.

Business Cards: Want to let the neighbors know about your summer lawn service? Maybe you would like to pick up extra babysitting jobs. Create your own business cards and personalize them with a photo! Many office supply stores sell business card paper. You can use a template to help you fit the text and image on your business card. A template is a document or file that has already been formatted for a specific purpose. The margins, columns, and other features are already in place.

CUSTOM LAWN CARE SERVICE

cell: 123-456-7890

Mike Smith

You can make business cards for any job you can think of.

Anna White

Certified Babysitter

cell: 123-456-7890

123 South Sun Street
Chicago, IL 60601

Slideshows: Another popular tool for sharing information is a slideshow. Slideshows can be made using Microsoft's PowerPoint or Apple's Keynote. Both programs have templates that make it easy to display information. How can you use digital images in a slideshow?

Many slides have placeholders for images. A placeholder is a box on the slide that shows where the image should appear. You insert the image in the placeholder.

You can use digital images to tell a story in other ways, too. With movie editing software, such as Windows Movie Maker or iMovie, you can import digital photos.

Once your slideshow is done, you can share it with your friends.

Then you can add your own narration to create a digital story or slideshow. Follow the directions for the specific software you are using. Here's a basic guide:

1. Plan ahead. Every good story has a beginning, middle, and end. Use a graphic organizer or storyboard to organize your photos and ideas. Write a draft of your narration. Be sure to add many details. Decide which part of the script will be read for each picture.

2. Next, import the photos into the movie software. Use your notes as a guide to place the images in the correct order.

3. Record your narration. Remember, good storytellers are lively when they speak.

4. As you play back the narration, adjust the display time for each photo. You'll want some photos to have a longer display time than others, depending on your script.

5. Add a title slide at the beginning. Be sure to include information about the creator on a credit slide, too.

6. Consider adding transitions between photos.

7. You have many options for saving and sharing your digital story files. They can be exported and viewed as QuickTime or Windows Media Player files or burned to DVDs.

CHAPTER FIVE

Closing Shots

Do you see digital images in a new light? They can really bring a project to life. But remember: Too much of a good thing is not so good at all! The last thing you want is for digital images to distract from your main ideas. Digital images and clip art should be used to enhance your project. Many times, less is more.

What kind of digital images will you use in your next project?

TRY THIS!

Are you putting the finishing touches on your project? You're not quite done yet! Think about your work. Ask yourself the following questions:

Don't write in the book!

Did I respect the intellectual property of others? When using scanned or online images, did I cite my sources? Did I request and receive permission to use any images protected by copyright?

YES   NO

Did I carefully select images that help make my assignments interesting?

YES   NO

continued ⟶

continued ———————→

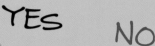

Digital images come in many sizes and packages. Did I think about how I want to use the images? Did I select image sizes and formats that fit my needs?

YES   NO

Did I take many photos? Did I explore the possibilities and try different editing tools and effects?

YES   NO

Did you answer yes to all of the questions? If so, congratulations! There's a good chance that you made great use of digital images. If you answered no to any questions, what changes can you make? Take the time to make final revisions. That's what expert information explorers do!

Practice and become a digital image pro. Get creative with your shots. Take chances with different editing tools. Go for it, and get the perfect shot!

TRY THIS!

It's time for some self-assessment. How can digital images be used as a tool for learning? Are they more useful for some projects than others? Can you think of ways to improve your skills and make the most of digital images? Maybe you are not comfortable using editing software. Could you spend some extra time getting familiar with the different editing tools? Finding your weaknesses is important. It helps you improve your skills and be the best learner you can be.

Keep practicing and soon you'll be a digital image pro!

Glossary

cite (SITE) give credit to the source of a fact, quote, image, or other information

cropping (KROP-ing) removing the edges from something, such as a photo

graphic organizer (GRAF-ik OR-guh-nye-zur) a visual representation that helps organize information and show relationships between ideas

intellectual property (in-tuh-LEK-choo-uhl PROP-ur-tee) an idea, invention, written work, or other creation of the mind that often has the potential to make money

keywords (KEE-wurdz) important words

mosaic (moh-ZAY-ik) a picture made up of small tiles or stones

pixels (PIKS-uhlz) small dots that make up a digital image

resolution (rez-uh-LOO-shuhn) a measurement of the number of pixels in a digital image

self-assessment (self-uh-SESS-muhnt) the process of rating your progress, strengths, and weaknesses and determining points that need improvement or changes you can make

Find Out More

BOOKS

Buckley, Annie. *Photography*. Ann Arbor, MI: Cherry Lake
    Publishing, 2009.

Gaines, Thom. *Digital Photo Madness!: 50 Weird & Wacky
    Things to Do with Your Digital Camera*. New York: Lark
    Books, 2010.

WEB SITES

GIMP—The GNU Image Manipulation Program

www.gimp.org/

GIMP is a free photo editing program.

National Geographic—Digital Photography Quick Tips

photography.nationalgeographic.com/photography/photo-tips/

digital-photography-quick-tips/

Find helpful tips for taking great digital photos.

Pics4Learning

www.pics4learning.com/

Find many digital images for school projects in this copyright-
friendly image collection for teachers and kids.

Index

About the Author

Suzy Rabbat is a National Board certified school librarian. She has two children, Mike and Annie. She lives in Mt. Prospect, Illinois, with her husband, Basile.